SCIENTOLOGY
Making the World a Better Place

C000255874

Founded and developed by L. Ron Hubb; religious philosophy which offers an exact rou ...yone can regain the truth and simplicity of his spiritual self.

Scientology consists of specific axioms that define the underlying causes and principles of existence and a vast area of observations in the humanities, a philosophic body that literally applies to the entirety of life.

This broad body of knowledge resulted in two applications of the subject: first, a technology for man to increase his spiritual awareness and attain the freedom sought by many great philosophic teachings; and, second, a great number of fundamental principles men can use to improve their lives. In fact, in this second application, Scientology offers nothing less than practical methods to better *every* aspect of our existence—means to create new ways of life. And from this comes the subject matter you are about to read.

Compiled from the writings of L. Ron Hubbard, the data presented here is but one of the tools which can be found in *The Scientology Handbook*. A comprehensive guide, the handbook contains numerous applications of Scientology which can be used to improve many other areas of life.

In this booklet, the editors have augmented the data with a short introduction, practical exercises and examples of successful application.

Courses to increase your understanding and further materials to broaden your knowledge are available at your nearest Scientology church or mission, listed at the back of this booklet.

Many new phenomena about man and life are described in Scientology, and so you may encounter terms in these pages you are not familiar with. These are described the first time they appear and in the glossary at the back of the booklet.

Scientology is for use. It is a practical philosophy, something one *does*. Using this data, you *can* change conditions.

Millions of people who want to do something about the conditions they see around them have applied this knowledge. They know that life can be improved. And they know that Scientology works.

Use what you read in these pages to help yourself and others and you will too.

CHURCH OF SCIENTOLOGY INTERNATIONAL

*T*he self-improvement shelves of bookstores, the airwaves and self-help speakers who travel the lecture circuit all offer myriad solutions to the problems of understanding life. Yet the endless stream of man's difficulties still do not resolve.

In this booklet, L. Ron Hubbard goes beneath all these "solutions" to provide the basic knowledge of what actually constitutes understanding.

What can you do with this knowledge? By knowing what understanding really is, you have the tools to handle life itself. This means that you have the tools to increase your understanding of just about anything—including the people you know and come into contact with.

This knowledge will enable you to help others who are experiencing the travails caused by misunderstandings, differing viewpoints, broken relationships and other ills that make man's life a string of successive hardships. You will learn the components of understanding, how they interrelate and bring about understanding. With the skills one can acquire from a study of the fundamentals contained herein, you can help bring others back into understanding with their fellow man and the world around them.

Although only a portion of the full technology Mr. Hubbard developed on this subject is contained here, it is enough to change your approach to life. And its use will help you flourish in any aspect of human activity.

If lack of understanding is, indeed, a source of man's problems, imagine his potentials without this hindrance. Millions of people who apply this knowledge are reaching heights they once only dreamed of— and are successfully assisting others to do the same.■

Affinity, Reality and Communication

T here are three factors in Scientology which are of the utmost importance in handling life. These three factors answer the questions: How should I talk to people? How can I give new ideas to people? How can I find what people are thinking about? How can I handle my work better?

These three factors in Scientology are called the ARC triangle. The abbreviation ARC (pronounced A-R-C rather than *arc*) is one of the most useful terms yet devised.

The ARC triangle is called a triangle because it has three related points. The first of these points is affinity. The second of these points is reality. The third of these points and the most important is communication.

These three factors are related. By affinity we mean emotional response. We mean the feeling of affection or lack of it, of emotion or misemotion (irrational or inappropriate emotion) connected with life. By reality we mean the solid objects, the *real* things of life. By communication we mean an interchange of ideas between two terminals (persons who can receive, relay or send a communication). Without affinity there is no reality or communication. Without reality there is no affinity or communication. Without communication there is neither affinity nor reality.

Application of the ARC triangle in the day-to-day circumstances one encounters in life requires an understanding of each of the triangle's components and their interrelationship.

Affinity is any emotional attitude which indicates the degree of liking for someone or something.

Reality is the degree of agreement reached by people. It also includes the solid objects, the real things of life.

Communication is the interchange of ideas across space.

Affinity

The first corner of the triangle is affinity.

The basic definition of *affinity* is the consideration of distance, whether good or bad. The most basic function of complete affinity would be the ability to occupy the same space as something else.

The word *affinity* is here used to mean love, liking or any other emotional attitude. Affinity is conceived in Scientology to be something of many facets. Affinity is a variable quality. *Affinity* is here used as a word with the context "degree of liking."

Man would not be man without affinity. Every animal has affinity to some degree, but man is capable of feeling an especially large amount. Long before he organized into cities, he had organized into tribes and clans. Before the tribes and clans there were undoubtedly packs. Man's instinctive need for affinity with his fellow human beings has long been recognized, and his domestication of other animals shows that this affinity extends also to other species. One could have guessed that the race which first developed affinity to its highest degree would become the dominant race on any planet and this has been borne out.

A child is full of affinity. Not only does he have affinity for his father, mother, brothers and sisters and his playmates but for his dogs, his cats and stray dogs that happen to come around. But affinity goes even beyond this. You can have a feeling of affinity for objects: "I love the way the grain stands out in that wood." There is a feeling of oneness with the earth, blue skies, rain, millponds, cartwheels and bullfrogs which is affinity.

Affinity is never identification (becoming one with another in feeling or interest) nor does it go quite so far as empathy (the power or state of imagining oneself to be another person and even share *his* ideas or feelings). You remain very much yourself when you have affinity for something but you also feel the essence of the thing for which you have affinity. You remain yourself and yet you draw closer to the object for which you have affinity. It is not a binding quality. There are no strings attached when affinity is given. To the receiver it carries no duties and no responsibilities. It is pure, easy and natural and flows out from the individual as easily as sunlight flows from the sun.

Affinity begets affinity. A person who is filled with the quality will automatically find people anywhere near him also beginning to be filled with affinity. It is a calming, warming, heartening influence on all who are capable of receiving and giving it.

One can readily observe the level of affinity between individuals or groups. For instance, two men talking with each other either are in affinity with each other or they aren't. If they are not, they will argue. If they are in affinity with each other, two other things have to be there: they have to have agreed upon a reality and they have to be able to communicate that reality to each other.

This brings us to the next corner: reality.

Reality

Reality could be defined as "that which appears to be." Reality is fundamentally agreement. What we agree to be real is real.

Reality, physical-universe reality, is sensed through various channels; we see something with our eyes, we hear something with our ears, we smell something with our nose, we touch something with our hands, and we decide, then, that there is something. But the only way we know it is through our senses and those senses are artificial channels. We are not in direct contact with the physical universe. We are in contact through our sense channels with it.

Those sense channels can be blunted. For instance, a man loses his eyesight, and as far as he is concerned there is no light or shape or color or depth perception to the physical universe. It still has a reality to him, but it is not the same reality as another person's. In other words, he is unable to conceive a physical universe completely without sight. One can't conceive these things without senses. So the physical universe is seen through these senses.

Two men can take a look at a table and agree it is a table. It is made out of wood, it is brown. The men agree to that. Of course, one understands that when he says "brown" and the other hears "brown," brown actually to the first man may be purple but he has agreed that it is brown because all his life people have been pointing to this color vibration and saying "brown." It might really be red to the second man, but he recognizes it as brown. So both men

Eyewitnesses at the scene of an accident or crime often present differing accounts of what occurred. Each person here has a different reality of what happened to a woman who had her purse snatched.

are in agreement although they might be seeing something different. But they agree this is brown, this is wood, this is a table. Now a third fellow walks in the door, comes up and takes a look at this thing and says, "Huh! An elephant!"

One man says, "It's a table, see? Elephants are ..."

"No, it's an elephant," replies the third man.

So the other two men say the third one is crazy. He doesn't agree with them. Do they attempt further to communicate with him? No. He doesn't agree with them. He has not agreed upon this reality. Are they in affinity with him? No. They say, "This guy is crazy." They don't like him. They don't want to be around him.

Now let's say two individuals are arguing, and one says, "That table is made out of wood," and the other says, "No, it is not. It's made out of metal which is painted to look like wood." They start arguing about this; they are trying to reach a point of agreement and they can't reach this point of agreement. Another fellow comes up and takes a look at the table and says, "As a matter of fact, the legs are painted to look like wood, but the top is wood and it is brown and it is a table." The first two men then reach an agreement. They feel an affinity. All of a sudden they feel friendly and they feel friendly toward the third man. He solved the problem. The two individuals have reached an agreement and go into communication.

For an individual, reality can only consist of his interpretation of the sensory perceptions he receives. The comparative unreliability of this data is clearly shown by the varying reports always received in the description of, say, an automobile accident. People who have studied this phenomenon report that there is an amazing degree of difference in the description given of the same scene by different observers. In other words, the reality of this situation differed in details for each of the observers. As a matter of fact, there is a wide area of agreement, extremely wide, the common agreement of mankind. This is the earth. We are men. The automobiles are automobiles. They are propelled by the explosion of certain chemicals. The air is the air. The sun is in the sky. There is usually an agreement that a wreck happened. Beyond this basic area of agreement there are differing interpretations of reality.

For all practical purposes, reality consists of your perception of it, and your perception of reality consists, to a large extent, of what you can communicate with other people.

Communication

The third and most important corner of the ARC triangle is communication. In human relationships this is more important than the other two corners of the triangle in understanding the composition of human relations in this universe. Communication is the solvent for all things. It dissolves all things.

How do people go into communication with each other?

In order for there to be communication, there must be agreement and affinity. In order for there to be affinity, there must be agreement on reality and communication. In order for there to be reality and agreement, there must be affinity and communication—one, two, three. If you knock affinity out, communication and reality go. If you knock reality out, communication and affinity will go. If you knock communication out, they will all go.

There are several ways to block a communication line (the route along which a communication travels from one person to another). One is to cut it, another one is to make it so painful that the person receiving it will cut it, and another one is to put so much on it that it jams. Those are three very important things to know about a communication line. Also, that communication must be *good* communication: the necessary data sent in the necessary direction and received.

All that communication will be about, by the way, is reality and affinity concerning the physical universe. Discussions will be whether there is or is not affinity, or whether there is or is not agreement and where the agreement is particularly disagreed with on the physical universe.

Affinity can be built up in a number of ways. You can talk to people and build up an affinity with them. But remember this is communication, not just talk. There are many, many ways to communicate. Two people can sit and look at each other and be in communication. One of the ways to go into communication is by tactile, the sense of touch. You can pet a cat, and the cat all of a sudden starts to purr; you are in communication with the cat. You can reach out and shake a person's hand and you are in communication with him because tactile has taken place. The old-school boys with the tooth-and-claw idea that "everybody hates everybody really, and everybody is on the defensive and that is why we have to force everybody into being social animals" said that the reason men shake hands is to show there is no weapon in the hand. No, it is a communication. In France, Italy, Spain and so forth they throw their arms around each other; there is lots of contact and that contact is communication.

If a person is badly out of communication and you reach out and pat him on the shoulder and he dodges slightly (he considers all things painful) even though he doesn't go on, you will find he is also out of communication vocally. You try to say something to him. "You know, I think that's a pretty

If one corner of the ARC triangle is knocked out the remaining corners also get knocked out. Here, a child cheerfully approaches his mother to give her flowers.

Preoccupied with housework, the mother ignores the child's communication, which becomes knocked out, followed soon after by less affinity and less reality.

good project, Project 342A, and I think we ought to go along with it." He will sit there and look at you and nod, and then he will go down and complete Project 36.

You say, "Project 36 has just been thrown out. We weren't going to go through with that at all," but he hardly knows you are talking to him. He dodges everything you say. Or he may talk to you so hard and so long you don't get a chance to tell him you want to do Project 342A. That is dodging you, too. In other words, he is out of communication with you. Therefore his affinity is low and he won't agree with you either. But if you can get him into agreement, communication will pick up and affinity will pick up.

This is about the most important data run across in the field of interpersonal relations.

You can take any group of men working on a project and take one look at the foreman and the men and tell whether or not these people are in communication with one another. If they aren't, they are not working as a coordinated team. They are not in communication, perhaps, because they are not agreed on what they are doing.

All you have to do is take the group, put them together and say, "What are you guys doing?" You don't ask the foreman, you ask the whole group and the foreman, "What are you guys doing?"

One fellow says, "I'm earning forty dollars a week. That's what I'm doing." Another one says, "Well, I'm glad to get out of the house every day. The old woman's pretty annoying." Another one says, "As a matter of fact, I occasionally get to drive the truck over there and I like to drive the truck, and I'll put up with the rest of this stuff. I drive the truck, and I've got to work anyhow." Another man might say, if he were being honest, "I'm staying on this job because I hate this dog that you've got here as a foreman. If I can devote my life to making him miserable, boy, that makes me happy."

All the time you thought that those men thought they were grading a road. Not one of them thought they were grading a road. You thought they were building a road. Not one of them was building a road; not one of them was even grading.

This crew may be unhappy and inefficient, but you get them together and you say, "Well, you know, some day a lot of cars will go over this road. Maybe they'll wreck themselves occasionally and so forth, but a lot of cars will go over this road. You boys are building a road. It's a pretty hard job, but somebody's got to do it. A lot of people will thank you boys for having built this road. I know you don't care anything about that, but that's really what we are doing around here. Now, I'd like a few suggestions from you people about how we could build this road a little bit better." All of a sudden the whole crew is building a road. Affinity, reality and communication go right up.

THE ARC TRIANGLE

Every point on the ARC triangle is dependent on the other two, and every two are dependent on one. One can't cut down one without cutting down the other two, and one can't rehabilitate one without rehabilitating the other two. On the positive side, one can rehabilitate any point on the triangle by rehabilitating any other point on it.

The interrelationship of the triangle becomes apparent at once when one asks, "Have you ever tried to talk to an angry man?" Without a high degree of liking and without some basis of agreement there is no communication. Without communication and some basis of emotional response there can be no reality. Without some basis for agreement and communication there can be no affinity. Thus we call these three things a triangle. Unless we have two corners of a triangle, there cannot be a third corner. Desiring any corner of the triangle, one must include the other two.

The triangle is not an equilateral triangle. Affinity and reality are very much less important than communication. It might be said that the triangle begins with communication, which brings into existence affinity and reality.

Since each of these three aspects of existence is dependent on the other two, anything which affects one of these will also similarly affect the others. It is very difficult to suffer a reversal of affinity without also suffering a blockage of communication and a consequent deterioration of reality.

Consider a lovers' quarrel: One of the pair offers affinity in a certain way to the other. This affinity is either reversed or not acknowledged. The first lover feels insulted and begins to break off communication. The second lover, not understanding this break-off, also feels insulted and makes the break in communication even wider. The area of agreement between the two inevitably diminishes and the reality of their relationship begins to go down. Since they no longer agree on reality, there is less possibility of affinity between them and the downward spiral goes on.

There are three ways of reversing this spiral. One is through raising of the necessity level of the individual. Another is by the intervention of some outside agency which will force the two lovers to agree or communicate. The third is by Scientology processing.

COMMUNICATION

UNDERSTANDING

REALITY **AFFINITY**

Affinity, reality and communication form the ARC triangle, with each point dependent upon the other two. These are the component parts of understanding.

Scientology processing is a precise, thoroughly codified activity with exact procedures. It is a very unique form of personal counseling which helps an individual look at his own existence and improves his ability to confront what he is and where he is.

Unless one of these three ways of reversing the spiral is utilized, eventually all of the reality of the relationship which had grown up between this pair of lovers would vanish and both of the people would be damaged in their total reality, their total ability to communicate, their total capacity for affinity.

Fortunately the spiral works both ways. Anything which will raise the level of affinity will also increase the ability to communicate and add to the perception of reality.

Falling in love is a good example of the raising of the ability to communicate and of a heightened sense of reality occasioned by a sudden increase in affinity. If it has happened to you, you will remember the wonderful smell of the air, the feeling of affection for the good solid ground, the way in which the stars seemed to shine brighter and the sudden new ability in expressing yourself.

If you have ever been alone, and in a dwindling spiral, only to have the telephone ring and the voice of a friend come across, you will have experienced the halting of a downward spiral through a lift in communication. This is particularly true if the friend happens to be a person with whom you converse easily and who seems to understand the communication which you try to give him. After such an experience, you are probably aware of a great deal more interest in the things around you (reality) and the increase of the feelings of affinity within you.

A troopship was slowly approaching the Golden Gate Bridge filled with troops who had been overseas for several months. As the ship slowly approached the bridge, all on board grew very quiet until at last no one was talking at all. Suddenly, as though by prearranged signal, just as the bow of the ship cleared the bridge, the men standing there broke into a tremendous cheer which carried on down the length of the ship as she went under the bridge. Suddenly everyone was talking to everyone excitedly. Men who scarcely knew each other were pounding each other on the back as though they were brothers. America regained some of its reality for these men and communication and affinity suddenly went up. Fast!

A person's ARC can be in a low state…

…but can be raised rapidly by communication from someone with whom ARC is high.

Affinity, reality and communication are part of everyday life—from a child going to school, through familial relations to governing a nation. And ignorance of their existence and application is equally as widespread; otherwise, one would not be continually swamped with the daily news of turmoil, strife and suffering due simply to lack of understanding.

However, knowledge of these components will only carry one so far. They must be applied. But how is that done?

How to Raise ARC

A principal application of ARC is to increase affinity, reality and communication, and thus understanding, between oneself and another. How does one talk to somebody else?

The way to do this is to establish <u>reality</u> by finding something with which you and the other person agree.

Then you attempt to maintain as high an affinity level as possible by knowing there is something you can like about him.

All three corners of the ARC triangle will have been established and you are then able to talk to him. Understanding will be possible because the three components of life—affinity, reality and communication—are present.

How to Use the ARC Triangle

Given these principles of the ARC triangle and its components, how would you talk to a man?

You cannot talk adequately to a man if you are in a subapathy (a state of disinterest below apathy) condition. In fact, you would not talk to him at all. You would have to have a little higher affinity than that to discuss things with anyone. Your ability to talk to any given man has to do with your emotional response to any given man. Anyone has different emotional responses to different people around him. In view of the fact that two terminals, or, that is to say, two people, are always involved in communication, one could see that someone else would have to be somewhat real. If one does not care about other people at all, one will have a great deal of difficulty talking to them, that is certain. The way to talk to a man, then, would be to find something to like about him and to discuss something with which he can agree. This is the downfall of most new ideas: One does not discuss subjects with which the other person has any point of agreement at all. And we come to a final factor with regard to reality.

That with which we agree tends to be more real than that with which we do not agree. There is a definite coordination between agreement and reality. Those things are real which we agree are real. Those things are not real which we agree are not real. On those things upon which we disagree we have very little reality. An experiment based on this would be an even joking discussion between two men of a third man who is present. The two men agree on something with which the third man cannot agree. The third man will drop in emotional tone and will actually become less real to the two people who are discussing him.

How do you talk to a man then? You establish reality by finding something with which you both agree. Then you attempt to maintain as high an affinity level as possible by knowing there is something you can like about him. And you are then able to talk with him. If you do not have the first two conditions, it is fairly certain that the third condition will not be present, which is to say, you will not be able to talk to him easily.

Affinity, reality and communication are interdependent one upon the other, and when one drops the other two drop also. When one rises the other two rise also. It is only necessary to improve one corner of this very valuable triangle in Scientology in order to improve the remaining two corners. It is only necessary to improve two corners of the triangle to improve the third.

Understanding

Understanding is compounded of affinity, reality and communication. When an individual's understanding is great, his ARC is quite high, and when an individual's ability to understand is small, his ARC is accordingly small.

When we have raised these three parts we have raised somebody's understanding. It is use of the ARC triangle which accomplishes this.

This triangle is the keystone of living associations. It is the common denominator of all life activities. Its use means a greater understanding of life itself.■

PRACTICAL EXERCISES

The following exercises will help you understand ARC better and increas
your ability to apply it.

1 Look around the environment and spot ten instances where a
individual is displaying affinity.

2 Look around the environment and spot ten examples where two or mor
individuals have reality on something.

3 Look around the environment and spot ten examples of communicatior

4 Spot more examples of affinity, reality and communication, noticin
how they interrelate. Continue to spot examples of affinity, reality an
communication as above until you clearly see the relationship betwee
these and are sure that each depends on the other two.

5 Using the data you have learned about the ARC triangle, raise the realit
between yourself and another person. Establish reality by findin
something with which you and the other person agree. Repeat this witl
different people as many times as needed until you can raise realit
between yourself and another with ease.

6 Using the data you have learned about the ARC triangle, increase the
affinity between yourself and another person. Find something you can like
about the person, and note the difference in affinity you have for the
person as a result. Repeat this with different people as many times as
needed until you can raise affinity between yourself and another with ease

7 Using the data you have learned about the ARC triangle, raise the
communication level between yourself and another person. Repeat this
with other people, over and over, until you are confident you can raise
the communication level between yourself and others.

8 Using the data you have learned about the ARC triangle, raise the ARC
between yourself and another person. Repeat this with other people,
over and over, until you are confident you can raise ARC between
yourself and others.

RESULTS FROM APPLICATION

Those who know and use the components of understanding—affinity, reality and communication—gain control over situations that, without this knowledge, could leave them impotent to act. The mechanics of ARC are simple yet powerful when used to resolve aspects of life.

In dealing with others, whether it be creating new relationships, maintaining good relationships or repairing those that have gone awry, the use of the ARC triangle is *the* key that unlocks previously closed doors to harmony and understanding.

Lovers' spats, relatives who won't speak to one for years, angry bosses, "natural" antipathies, the generation gap, all dissolve under the soothing balm of ARC. Once learned, the use of the ARC triangle is never forgotten or left unused; it swiftly becomes a way of handling life. Those who use it say they couldn't imagine surviving without. That it is one of the "ABCs" of life is reflected in the examples that follow.

A court reporter in Los Angeles was having tremendous difficulty getting along with her parents. She had upset them and, consequently, could no longer face them and had stopped communicating with them. Her father sent letters which expressed upset with her and which, in turn, upset her immensely since she loved and respected her parents. A friend came along about this time and showed her L. Ron Hubbard's materials on ARC to help her with this situation. Here is what came to pass:

"My parents and I had become more and more estranged. This data from Mr. Hubbard showed me exactly what was wrong and gave me a very easy-to-apply solution. I was able to communicate with my parents without upsetting them by establishing reality with them. After that, my dad wrote to me and for the first time ever in my life, said, 'I love you.' I could have died of happiness. Applying this data not only restored our relationship, it made it warmer than it had ever been."

The zing had gone out of the marriage of a couple with five children. A friend of theirs listened to the wife complaining that they no longer had anything in common and were drifting apart. She decided to do something to help both the children and the couple.

"To do something about this, I told my friend about the ARC triangle, and went over all the parts of it with her.

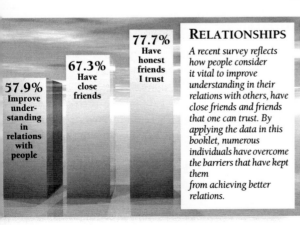

57.9% Improve under- standing in relations with people

67.3% Have close friends

77.7% Have honest friends I trust

RELATIONSHIPS

A recent survey reflects how people consider it vital to improve understanding in their relations with others, have close friends and friends that one can trust. By applying the data in this booklet, numerous individuals have overcome the barriers that have kept them from achieving better relations.

She realized that she and her husband were not in communication and had no common reality anymore. She was involved with raising her five children, while he was involved with work. It was quite different from when they courted as teenagers.

"So we worked out a solution. They went out, just the two of them. She used the tools of the ARC triangle to get in communication with her husband about points of common reality, which started with a movie that they had seen together. From that point, they got into further communication with one another and the marriage improved and continued to improve. It was really great to be able to use such a basic and simple tool to keep a family with five children together."

In Los Angeles, a young woman had a troubled relationship with her brother. Since childhood they had always picked on each other, clashing constantly. Her brother had become involved with hard drugs and grew more and more critical of others. The woman, after learning some of the fundamental principles about affinity, reality and communication in Scientology, decided to handle this relationship and his criticism of her and life in general. She applied her new skills and got into communication with him.

"I applied what I had learned about communication and found the exact thing ruining his life. He had been one of the most promising athletes in his high-school years, but had failed to follow through on his goals. He told me that he wanted to have things to strive for in life and that he wanted to

achieve them. He realized when talking me that the abandonment of his goals h probably led him into doing drugs in t first place. After that, my brother handl his drug problem and began to take ev more positive actions to improve his life. previously had gone from one relationship another for years, but after that, he actua settled down and got married. O relationship improved from that point a he now respects me for what I do."

By the end of high school, a youn man had transformed from being extroverted, happy teenager to introverted and miserable one. Abiliti he had enjoyed previously, such as t simple ability to help people just listening to them, and a native ability cheer people up and make them feel go about themselves—all of these seemed have vanished by the time he graduate school. He was using drugs and w confused and losing.

"I thought I would never get tho abilities back. Then I found Scientology, a things changed. I learned about a ve simple but powerful principle known as t ARC triangle. Anyone can use this princip in day-to-day living. I found that with i I could improve any part of my life. learned exactly how to use communicatic with other people to increase affinity a reality and bring about understanding. works. I can help people as never befo through my new understanding communication and the ARC triangle. The is such a thing as real help, and real hope, long as Scientology is in use by people lil you and I. But don't listen to me—read L. Ron Hubbard's books and see for yourself!"

An electrician found that the upsets and misunderstandings that can arise in working closely with others could cut not only his efficiency, but his satisfaction with his work. Using the principle of the ARC triangle brought a welcome change for the better.

"I used to have trouble trying to deal with many of my customers and fellow workers. I just 'didn't get along with them.' I thought this was just the way life was, and though I didn't like it, there didn't seem to be anything I could do about it. I don't know how much time I wasted with arguments, lack of cooperation and misunderstandings. Not to mention the slowdowns that can happen when people who are supposed to be working **together** don't get along. It seems like anything that can go wrong in such circumstances **does** go wrong, and that makes matters worse.

"I've found repeatedly that when I dislike someone, if I take the time to get into communication with the person, no matter how 'minor' or 'unimportant' the subject, the dislike diminishes or just vanishes completely. It works like magic. This is important in my work, where I come into contact with quite a lot of people.

"Being able to prevent upsets and disagreements, or handle them if they do come up, is invaluable. It has saved me hundreds and hundreds of hours that otherwise would have gone to waste. And I couldn't even begin to measure the stress, personal bad feelings and upset it's saved me **and** others. A definite bonus!"

A Medford, Oregon woman handled an uncomfortable situation in her family with ease, using the ARC triangle.

"For years my brother and sister and I dreaded visiting our mother. The reason? She would insist that we listen to her long, drawn out and detailed commentary on the latest article or book she was reading, then expect us to add our own views or comments. We didn't dare disagree with her or it would cause a big upset. We decided the best thing to do was just to stay away.

"After studying Mr. Hubbard's data on the ARC triangle, I realized that Mother was just trying to establish some reality between us. She was lacking anyone to agree with her, so her ARC had gone down to a very low point. The next time I saw her I made it a point to listen well to what she had to say, then let her know that I really did understand what she was talking about. It worked like magic! The reality went up, the affinity went way up and we were able to carry on with some very good communication for the first time in years.

"I told my brother and sister what I'd done and why. Now we have no problem in communicating with our mother and we're all very much happier for it."

A major improvement in her relationship with her father was an English girl's reward for putting the technology of ARC to work.

"A few months ago I saw my father after I'd been away from home for several years. The last time I'd seen him I was pretty young and I had never really had much of a meaningful conversation with him. This time, I had the technology of ARC and I applied it as we talked.

"Though he was happy to see me, it was obvious there was something troubling him so I got the conversation around to how he was **really** doing. He told me some of the troubles he had run into. This raised my reality of what was bothering him, and I let him know I could really understand the scene.

"Just with that simple action he gave a great sigh of relief, sat up straighter in his seat and looked a lot brighter—like life wasn't so impossible to live anymore. I would swear he looked at least two years younger! I don't think anyone had actually understood his communication and acknowledged it in a long time.

"For the remaining few days of our visit, we could talk about anything, just like talking with an old friend. Our reality and affinity for each other soared. It was great!"

The principle of the ARC triangle forms the basis for any close relationship, as a Philadelphia woman experienced:

"Shortly after I began studying Scientology I had a remarkable experience that demonstrated to me the power of the ARC triangle.

"I made a new friend, a person who had done some professional training in Scientology counseling technology. I w[as] amazed at this person's ability [to] communicate. It was beyond anything [I] had experienced.

"We became very good friends and [I] was able to talk to him as I had never talke[d] to anyone before. I **knew** he understoo[d] what I had to say. Once I let him know [I] needed to tell him something that to me w[as] very important and very difficult to tal[k] about. He took me to a quiet place and the[n] waited patiently as I got my courage up t[o] be able to say it. I told him and the[n] experienced from him the most perfe[ct] acknowledgment I could have imagined.

"It was totally clear to me that he ha[d] reality on what I'd said and that h[e] understood it perfectly. And of course th[e] affinity between us at that point wa[s] tremendous. I appreciated him and hi[s] ability beyond belief. It was anothe[r] demonstration for me of the power of th[e] ARC triangle."

Knowing that communication is th[e] universal solvent and that real friendshi[p] is based on ARC, a German Boy Scou[t] was able to resolve an upset that ha[d] shattered his friendship with another boy[.]

"I had a very good friend who was i[n] the same Boy Scout troop and he decided t[o] leave the group. I was very upset with hi[m] and was not willing to have much to do wit[h] him anymore; on the other hand I was sa[d] because we had been very good friends.

"One afternoon his brother wanted t[o] go to the movies with the two of us.

"I reluctantly agreed, then decided Okay. I am just going to get back into ARC with him and find out exactly what happened and tell him honestly how it upset me when he left our scout group.'

"I told him all that and immediately felt much better. He explained to me why he had made that decision. I could now understand what had happened because my reality had increased through communication. Once we had this upset cleared out of the way we were the best of friends again."

A student at Barcelona University was having considerable difficulty dealing with people and situations. His solution was to withdraw from life—until he found out about the interrelationship of affinity, reality and communication.

"I first learned about ARC several years ago when I was attending university. I realized that I was able to communicate, but my communication was lacking affinity. When I understood what affinity was, I started to put more in my communication with others and to look at them from another viewpoint.

"I immediately saw that the affinity that I was putting there was coming back multiplied by ten. It might seem something normal, but for me it was quite miraculous. I used to mind my own business and didn't talk too much with people; however, after reading about ARC, I was getting in real communication and exchange of ideas and feelings with other people.

"The funny thing is that I started to gain more and more reality about myself and others and got to a point where I was in control of any situation I was facing.

"I started to get done what I wanted to get done, and my ability to predict what was going to happen became something amazing to me. I started to communicate with the individuals of my class and to get a constructive viewpoint; people would come to me to congratulate me just for the mere fact of communicating and putting some purpose in the normally apathetic course rooms of the university.

"Before having any idea of the ARC triangle my viewpoint was that the best solution to all my problems was to become a hermit, get lost in an isolated farm, or in a classroom teaching literature, and ignore what is going on in this world. From an introverted and passive attitude I changed to one that is positive and dynamic. Just by understanding what affinity is. I feel affinity for people and I feel affinity for this planet. And I know that if more persons understand this data we will be able to create a place where all can be truly happy. Which, after all, is what we all want."

ABOUT
L. RON HUBBARD

No more fitting statement typifies the life of L. Ron Hubbard than his simple declaration: "I like to help others and count it as my greatest pleasure in life to see a person free himself from the shadows which darken his days." Behind these pivotal words stands a lifetime of service to mankind and a legacy of wisdom that enables anyone to attain long-cherished dreams of happiness and spiritual freedom.

Born in Tilden, Nebraska on March 13, 1911, his road of discovery and dedication to his fellows began at an early age. "I wanted other people to be happy, and could not understand why they weren't," he wrote of his youth; and therein lay the sentiments that would long guide his steps. By the age of nineteen, he had traveled more than a quarter of a million miles, examining the cultures of Java, Japan, India and the Philippines.

Returning to the United States in 1929, Ron resumed his formal education and studied mathematics, engineering and the then new field of nuclear physics—all providing vital tools for continued research. To finance that research, Ron embarked upon a literary career in the early 1930s, and soon became one of the most widely read authors of popular fiction. Yet never losing sight of his primary goal, he continued his mainline research through extensive travel and expeditions.

With the advent of World War II, he entered the United States Navy as a lieutenant (junior grade) and served as commander of antisubmarine corvettes. Left partially blind and lame from injuries sustained during combat, he was diagnosed as permanently disabled by 1945. Through application of his theories on the mind, however, he was not only able to help fellow servicemen, but also to regain his own health.

After five more years of intensive research, Ron's discoveries were presented to the world in *Dianetics: The Modern Science of Mental Health*. The first popular handbook on the human mind expressly written for the man in the street, *Dianetics* ushered in a new era of hope for mankind and a new

phase of life for its author. He did, however, not cease his research, and as breakthrough after breakthrough was carefully codified through late 1951, the applied religious philosophy of Scientology was born.

Because Scientology explains the whole of life, there is no aspect of man's existence that L. Ron Hubbard's subsequent work did not address. Residing variously in the United States and England, his continued research brought forth solutions to such social ills as declining educational standards and pandemic drug abuse.

All told, L. Ron Hubbard's works on Scientology and Dianetics total forty million words of recorded lectures, books and writings. Together, these constitute the legacy of a lifetime that ended on January 24, 1986. Yet the passing of L. Ron Hubbard in no way constituted an end; for with a hundred million of his books in circulation and millions of people daily applying his technologies for betterment, it can truly be said the world still has no greater friend.■

GLOSSARY

acknowledge: give (someone) an acknowledgment. *See also* **acknowledgment** in this glossary.

acknowledgment: something said or done to inform another that his statement or action has been noted, understood and received.

affinity: love, liking or any other emotional attitude; the degree of liking. The basic definition of affinity is the consideration of distance, whether good or bad.

ARC triangle: a triangle which is a symbol of the fact that *affinity, reality* and *communication* act together to bring about understanding. No point of the triangle can be raised without also raising the other two points, and no point of it can be lowered without also lowering the other two points.

communication: an interchange of ideas across space between two individuals.

communication line: the route along which a communication travels from one person to another.

confront: to face without flinching or avoiding. The ability to confront is actually the ability to be there comfortably and perceive.

misemotion: irrational or inappropriate emotion. It is a coined word taken from *mis-* (wrong) + *emotion.* To say that a person was *misemotional* would indicate that the person did not display the emotion called for by the actual circumstances of the situation. Being

misemotional would be synonymous wi being irrational. One can fairly judge t rationality of any individual by the corre ness of the emotion he displays in a given s of circumstances. To be joyful and hap when circumstances call for joy and hap ness would be rational. To display gr without sufficient present time cause wou be irrational.

processing: a special form of person counseling, unique in Scientology, whic helps an individual look at his own exi ence and improves his ability to confro what he is and where he is. Processing is precise, thoroughly codified activity wi exact procedures.

reality: that which appears to be. Reali is fundamentally agreement; the degree agreement reached by people. What v agree to be real is real.

Scientology: an applied religious philos phy developed by L. Ron Hubbard. It is th study and handling of the spirit in relatio ship to itself, universes and other life. Th word *Scientology* comes from the Latin *sci* which means "know" and the Greek wor *logos,* meaning "the word or outward for by which the inward thought is expresse and made known." Thus, Scientology mear knowing about knowing.

terminal: a person, point or position whic can receive, relay or send a communication

CHURCHES OF SCIENTOLOGY

Contact Your Nearest Church or Organization or visit www.volunteerministers.org

UNITED STATES

ALBUQUERQUE
Church of Scientology
106 Menaul Boulevard NE
Albuquerque, New Mexico 87110

ANN ARBOR
Church of Scientology
6 E. Michigan Avenue
Battle Creek, Michigan 49017

ATLANTA
Church of Scientology
1611 Mt. Vernon Road
Dunwoody, Georgia 30338

AUSTIN
Church of Scientology
2200 Guadalupe
Austin, Texas 78705

BOSTON
Church of Scientology
448 Beacon Street
Boston, Massachusetts 02115

BUFFALO
Church of Scientology
47 West Huron Street
Buffalo, New York 14202

CHICAGO
Church of Scientology
3011 North Lincoln Avenue
Chicago, Illinois 60657-4207

CINCINNATI
Church of Scientology
215 West 4th Street, 5th Floor
Cincinnati, Ohio 45202-2670

CLEARWATER
Church of Scientology
Flag Service Organization
210 South Fort Harrison Avenue
Clearwater, Florida 33756

Foundation Church of
Scientology
Flag Ship Service Organization
c/o *Freewinds* Relay Office
118 North Fort Harrison Avenue
Clearwater, Florida 33755-4013

COLUMBUS
Church of Scientology
30 North High Street
Columbus, Ohio 43215

DALLAS
Church of Scientology
Celebrity Centre Dallas
1850 North Buckner Boulevard
Dallas, Texas 75228

DENVER
Church of Scientology
3385 South Bannock Street
Englewood, Colorado 80110

DETROIT
Church of Scientology
28000 Middlebelt Road
Farmington Hills, Michigan
48334

HONOLULU
Church of Scientology
1146 Bethel Street
Honolulu, Hawaii 96813

KANSAS CITY
Church of Scientology
3619 Broadway
Kansas City, Missouri 64111

LAS VEGAS
Church of Scientology
846 East Sahara Avenue
Las Vegas, Nevada 89104

Church of Scientology
Celebrity Centre Las Vegas
4850 W. Flamingo Road, Ste. 10
Las Vegas, Nevada 89103

LONG ISLAND
Church of Scientology
99 Railroad Station Plaza
Hicksville, New York 11801-2850

LOS ANGELES AND VICINITY
Church of Scientology
of Los Angeles
4810 Sunset Boulevard
Los Angeles, California 90027

Church of Scientology
1451 Irvine Boulevard
Tustin, California 92680

Church of Scientology
1277 East Colorado Boulevard
Pasadena, California 91106

Church of Scientology
15643 Sherman Way
Van Nuys, California 91406

Church of Scientology
American Saint Hill
Organization
1413 L. Ron Hubbard Way
Los Angeles, California 90027

Church of Scientology
American Saint Hill Foundation
1413 L. Ron Hubbard Way
Los Angeles, California 90027

Church of Scientology
Advanced Organization
of Los Angeles
1306 L. Ron Hubbard Way
Los Angeles, California 90027

Church of Scientology
Celebrity Centre International
5930 Franklin Avenue
Hollywood, California 90028

LOS GATOS
Church of Scientology
2155 South Bascom Avenue,
Suite 120
Campbell, California 95008

MIAMI
Church of Scientology
120 Giralda Avenue
Coral Gables, Florida 33134

MINNEAPOLIS
Church of Scientology
Twin Cities
1011 Nicollet Mall
Minneapolis, Minnesota 55403

MOUNTAIN VIEW
Church of Scientology
2483 Old Middlefield Way
Mountain View, California 94043

NASHVILLE
Church of Scientology
Celebrity Centre Nashville
1204 16th Avenue South
Nashville, Tennessee 37212

NEW HAVEN
Church of Scientology
909 Whalley Avenue
New Haven, Connecticut
06515-1728

NEW YORK CITY
Church of Scientology
227 West 46th Street
New York, New York 10036-1409

Church of Scientology
Celebrity Centre New York
65 East 82nd Street
New York, New York 10028

ORLANDO
Church of Scientology
1830 East Colonial Drive
Orlando, Florida 32803-4729

PHILADELPHIA
Church of Scientology
1315 Race Street
Philadelphia, Pennsylvania 19107

PHOENIX
Church of Scientology
2111 West University Drive
Mesa, Arizona 85201

PORTLAND
Church of Scientology
2636 NE Sandy Boulevard
Portland, Oregon 97232-2342

Church of Scientology
Celebrity Centre Portland
708 SW Salmon Street
Portland, Oregon 97205

SACRAMENTO
Church of Scientology
825 15th Street
Sacramento, California
95814-2096

SALT LAKE CITY
Church of Scientology
1931 South 1100 East
Salt Lake City, Utah 84106

SAN DIEGO
Church of Scientology
1330 4th Avenue
San Diego, California 92101

SAN FRANCISCO
Church of Scientology
83 McAllister Street
San Francisco, California 94102

SAN JOSE
Church of Scientology
80 East Rosemary Street
San Jose, California 95112

SANTA BARBARA
Church of Scientology
524 State Street
Santa Barbara, California 93101

SEATTLE
Church of Scientology
2226 3rd Avenue
Seattle, Washington 98121

ST. LOUIS
Church of Scientology
6901 Delmar Boulevard
University City, Missouri 63130

TAMPA
Church of Scientology
3617 Henderson Boulevard
Tampa, Florida 33609-4501

WASHINGTON, DC
Founding Church of Scientology
of Washington, DC
1701 20th Street NW
Washington, DC 20009

PUERTO RICO

HATO REY
Dianetics Center of Puerto Rico
272 JT Piñero Avenue
Hyde Park
San Juan, Puerto Rico 00918

CANADA

EDMONTON
Church of Scientology
10206 106th Street NW
Edmonton, Alberta
Canada T5J 1H7

KITCHENER
Church of Scientology
104 King Street West, 2nd Floor
Kitchener, Ontario
Canada N2G 1A6

MONTREAL
Church of Scientology
4489 Papineau Street
Montreal, Quebec
Canada H2H 1T7

OTTAWA
Church of Scientology
150 Rideau Street, 2nd Floor
Ottawa, Ontario
Canada K1N 5X6

QUEBEC
Church of Scientology
350 Bd Chareste Est
Quebec, Quebec
Canada G1K 3H5

TORONTO
Church of Scientology
696 Yonge Street, 2nd Floor
Toronto, Ontario
Canada M4Y 2A7

VANCOUVER
Church of Scientology
401 West Hastings Street
Vancouver, British Columbia
Canada V6B 1L5

WINNIPEG
Church of Scientology
315 Garry Street, Suite 210
Winnipeg, Manitoba
Canada R3B 2G7

UNITED KINGDOM

BIRMINGHAM
Church of Scientology
8 Ethel Street
Winston Churchill House
Birmingham, England B2 4BG

BRIGHTON
Church of Scientology
Third Floor, 79-83 North Street
Brighton, Sussex
England BN1 1ZA

EAST GRINSTEAD
Church of Scient ology
Saint Hill Foundation
Saint Hill Manor
East Grinstead, West Sussex
England RH19 4JY

Advanced Organization
Saint Hill
Saint Hill Manor
East Grinstead, West Sussex
England RH19 4JY

EDINBURGH
Hubbard Academy of Personal
Independence
20 Southbridge
Edinburgh, Scotland EH1 1LL

LONDON
Church of Scientology
68 Tottenham Court Road
London, England W1P 0BB

Church of Scientology
Celebrity Centre London
42 Leinster Gardens
London, England W2 3AN

MANCHESTER
Church of Scientology
258 Deansgate
Manchester, England M3 4BG

PLYMOUTH
Church of Scientology
41 Ebrington Street
Plymouth, Devon
England PL4 9AA

SUNDERLAND
Church of Scientology
51 Fawcett Street
Sunderland, Tyne and Wear
England SR1 1RS

AUSTRALIA

ADELAIDE
Church of Scientology
24–28 Waymouth Street
Adelaide, South Australia
Australia 5000

BRISBANE
Church of Scientology
106 Edward Street, 2nd Floor
Brisbane, Queensland
Australia 4000

CANBERRA
Church of Scientology
43–45 East Row
Canberra City, ACT
Australia 2601

MELBOURNE
Church of Scientology
42–44 Russell Street
Melbourne, Victoria
Australia 3000

PERTH
Church of Scientology
108 Murray Street, 1st Floor
Perth, Western Australia
Australia 6000

SYDNEY
Church of Scientology
201 Castlereagh Street
Sydney, New South Wales
Australia 2000

Church of Scientology
Advanced Organization
Saint Hill Australia,
New Zealand and Oceania
19–37 Greek Street
Glebe, New South Wales
Australia 2037

NEW ZEALAND

AUCKLAND
Church of Scientology
159 Queen Street, 3rd Floor
Auckland 1, New Zealand

BUILD A BETTER WORLD

BECOME A VOLUNTEER MINISTER

Help bring happiness, purpose and truth to your fellow man. Become a Volunteer Minister.

Thousands of Volunteer Ministers bring relief and sanity to others all over the world using techniques like the ones found in this booklet. But more help is needed. Your help.

As a Volunteer Minister you can today handle things which seemed impossible yesterday. And you can vastly improve this world's tomorrow.

Become a Volunteer Minister and brighten the world to a better place for you to live. It's easy to do. For help and information about becoming a Volunteer Minister, visit our website today. www.volunteerministers.org

You can also call or write your nearest Volunteer Ministers International organization.

VOLUNTEER MINISTERS INTERNATIONAL
A DEPARTMENT OF THE INTERNATIONAL HUBBARD ECCLESIASTICAL LEAGUE OF PASTORS

INTERNATIONAL OFFICE
6331 Hollywood Boulevard, Suite 708
Los Angeles, California 90028
Tel: (323) 960-3560 (800) 435-7498

WESTERN US
1308 L. Ron Hubbard Way
Los Angeles, California 90027
Tel: (323) 953-3357
1-888-443-5760
ihelpwestus@earthlink.net

EASTERN US
349 W. 48th Street
New York, New York 10036
Tel: (212) 757-9610
1-888-443-5788

CANADA
696 Yonge Street
Toronto, Ontario
Canada M4Y 2A7
Tel: (416) 968-0070

LATIN AMERICA
Federación Mexicana de
Dianética, A.C.
Puebla #31
Colonia Roma, CP 06700
Mexico, D.F.
Tel: 525-511-4452

EUROPE
Store Kongensgade 55
1264 Copenhagen K
Denmark
Tel: 45-33-737-322

ITALY
Via Cadorna, 61
20090 Vimodrone (MI)
Italy
Tel: 39-0227-409-246

AUSTRALIA
201 Castlereagh Street
3rd Floor
Sydney, New South Wales
Australia 2000
Tel: 612-9267-6422

AFRICA
6th Floor, Budget House
130 Main Street
Johannesburg 2001
South Africa
Tel: 083-331-7170

UNITED KINGDOM
Saint Hill Manor
East Grinstead, West Sussex
England RH19 4JY
Tel: 44-1342-301-895

HUNGARY
1438 Budapest
PO Box 351, Hungary
Tel: 361-321-5298

COMMONWEALTH OF INDEPENDENT STATES
c/o Hubbard Humanitarian
Center
Ul. Borisa Galushkina 19A
129301 Moscow, Russia
Tel: 7-095-961-3414

TAIWAN
2F, 65, Sec. 4
Ming-Sheng East Road
Taipei, Taiwan ROC
Tel: 88-628-770-5074

www.volunteerministers.org

NEW ERA Publications International ApS
Store Kongensgade 53, 1264 Copenhagen K, Denmark
ISBN 87-7968-391-6

NEW ERA is a registered trademark owned by NEW ERA Publications International.

Bridge Publications, Inc. is a registered trademark and service mark in California and it is owned by Bridge Publications, Inc.

Printed by NEW ERA Publications International ApS

An L. RON HUBBARD Publication